LONG-TERM INVESTING:

A GUIDE TO INVESTING IN REAL ESTATE RENTALS

Table of Contents

Introduction

Chapter 1: Understanding Real Estate Investment

- Cash flow, ROI, cap rate, and more
- The Real Estate Market Cycle
  - Phases of the market and how they affect investments

Chapter 2: Developing Your Investment Strategy

- Setting Investment Goals
  - Short-term vs. long-term objectives
  - Financial independence and retirement planning
- Risk Tolerance and Diversification
  - Balancing risk and return
  - Geographic and property type diversification

Chapter 3: Financing Your Real Estate Investment

- Understanding Financing Options
  - Conventional loans, FHA loans, and VA loans

- Alternative financing: seller financing, hard money loans
- Building a Strong Credit Profile
  - Importance of credit score and debt-to-income ratio
- Calculating Affordability and Loan Terms
  - Down payments, interest rates, and loan terms

Chapter 4: Finding and Evaluating Properties

- Researching the Market
  - Analyzing local markets and trends
  - Tools and resources for market research
- Property Evaluation Criteria
  - Location, condition, and potential for appreciation
  - Conducting a thorough property inspection
- Working with Real Estate Agents and Brokers

- Finding the right professionals to assist you

Chapter 5: Analyzing Investment Properties

- Financial Analysis Tools
  - Calculating cash flow and profitability
  - Understanding net operating income (NOI) and cap rate
- Investment Metrics
  - Return on investment (ROI) and internal rate of return (IRR)
- Case Studies and Examples
  - Real-life examples of successful rental investments

Chapter 6: Managing Rental Properties

- Property Management Options
  - Self-management vs. hiring a property manager

- o Protecting your investment with insurance

Chapter 8: Scaling Your Real Estate Portfolio

- Strategies for Growth
  - o Reinvesting profits and leveraging equity
  - o Partnerships and joint ventures
- Portfolio Management
  - o Balancing different types of properties
  - o Diversifying across markets

Conclusion

- Building Long-Term Wealth with Real Estate
  - o The power of compound growth and passive income

- Continuing Education and Resources
  - Recommended books, courses, and online communities
- Final Thoughts and Encouragement

Appendices

- Glossary of Terms
- Useful Resources and Tools
- Sample Financial Analysis Worksheets
- Checklist for Property Evaluation

Long-Term Wealth: A Guide to Investing in Real Estate Rentals

Introduction

Why Invest in Real Estate?

Real estate has long been a cornerstone of wealth building and financial independence. Investing in long-term rentals offers unique benefits that can provide stability and passive income for years to come. Unlike other investment options, such as stocks, real estate tends to appreciate in value over time, offering both immediate cash flow and long-term capital growth.

Real estate also comes with significant tax advantages, such as depreciation and deductible expenses, which can enhance returns. Historically, real estate has shown resilience during economic downturns, making it a reliable component of a diversified investment portfolio.

Who is This Book For?

This book is designed for anyone interested in building wealth through real estate. Whether you are a beginner curious about entering the market or an experienced investor seeking to diversify your holdings, this guide will provide you with practical strategies and insights. If you're planning for retirement or looking to generate passive income, real estate can be an effective vehicle to achieve those goals.

Chapter 1: Understanding Real Estate Investment

Types of Real Estate Investments

Investing in real estate can take many forms. Primarily, it's important to differentiate between residential and commercial properties. Residential real estate includes single-family homes, duplexes, and multi-family properties. These properties are often more accessible to individual investors and can provide steady rental income.

Commercial properties, such as office buildings, retail spaces, and industrial properties, typically require a larger initial investment but can offer higher returns. They also come with more complex management needs and greater exposure to economic cycles.

Within residential investments, the choice between single-family homes and multi-family properties is significant. Single-family homes often attract more stable, long-term tenants, while multi-family properties can generate higher overall income but may require more hands-on management.

Key Real Estate Investment Terms

Before diving deeper, it's crucial to understand some key real estate investment terms:

- **Cash Flow**: The net income from a property after all expenses have been paid. Positive cash flow is essential for a successful rental investment.

- **Return on Investment (ROI)**: A measure of the profitability of an investment, calculated as a percentage of the initial investment cost.
- **Cap Rate (Capitalization Rate)**: A metric used to evaluate the return potential of a real estate investment, calculated by dividing the net operating income by the property's purchase price.

The Real Estate Market Cycle

Real estate markets move in cycles, typically consisting of four phases: expansion, peak, contraction, and recovery.

- **Expansion**: Characterized by growing demand and rising prices.

- **Peak**: When growth slows, and prices stabilize at high levels.
- **Contraction**: A period of declining demand and falling prices.
- **Recovery**: When the market begins to rebound from its lowest point.

Understanding where the market is in this cycle can help you make informed investment decisions and time your purchases effectively.

Chapter 2: Developing Your Investment Strategy

Setting Investment Goals

Clear investment goals are the foundation of a successful strategy. Are you seeking immediate cash flow or long-term appreciation? Is your primary goal financial independence or retirement planning? Defining these objectives will guide your decision-making process and help you choose the right properties.

Exercise: Write down your top three investment goals and the timeline in which you hope to achieve them.

Risk Tolerance and Diversification

Assessing your risk tolerance is crucial. Real estate is generally less volatile than stocks, but all investments carry some risk. Diversifying your real estate portfolio can help mitigate this risk. Consider investing in different property types and locations to balance potential returns with exposure.

Chapter 3: Financing Your Real Estate Investment

Understanding Financing Options

Securing the right financing is a critical step in the investment process. Here are some common options:

- **Conventional Loans**: These are typical bank loans with fixed or variable interest rates. They usually require a 20% down payment and are based on your creditworthiness.

- **FHA Loans**: Backed by the Federal Housing Administration, these loans require lower down payments and are ideal for first-time homebuyers.
- **VA Loans**: Available to veterans, these loans often require no down payment, making them an excellent choice for qualified individuals.
- **Alternative Financing**: Options like seller financing (where the seller provides the loan) and hard money loans (short-term, high-interest loans) can be useful for investors who may not qualify for traditional financing.

Building a Strong Credit Profile

A strong credit profile is essential for securing favorable loan terms. Your credit score and debt-to-income ratio are critical factors lenders consider.

Aim for a high credit score and low debt levels to improve your loan options. If your credit score needs improvement, consider strategies such as paying down existing debts and ensuring all bills are paid on time.

Calculating Affordability and Loan Terms

Understanding what you can afford is a crucial part of the investment process. Calculate your affordability by considering the down payment, interest rates, and loan terms. Use formulas to determine monthly payments and total costs over the life of the loan. Ensure that your expected rental income will cover these costs, along with other property-related expenses.

Example: Suppose you're considering a $300,000 property. With a 20% down payment and a 4% interest rate on a 30-year loan, your monthly mortgage payment would be approximately

$1,145. Ensure this payment is manageable within your budget and expected cash flow.

Chapter 4: Finding and Evaluating Properties

Researching the Market

Conducting thorough market research is essential to finding profitable investment properties. Analyze local market trends, including employment rates, population growth, and economic indicators. Use online tools like Zillow and Redfin to access market data and property listings.

Property Evaluation Criteria

When evaluating potential properties, consider:

- **Location**: The property's proximity to schools, workplaces, and amenities can significantly impact its desirability and rental income potential.
- **Condition**: Assess the physical state of the property. Determine renovation costs and factor them into your investment calculations.
- **Potential for Appreciation**: Investigate historical price trends and future development plans in the area.

Working with Real Estate Agents and Brokers

Partnering with a knowledgeable real estate agent or broker can greatly enhance your property search. Look for professionals with experience in investment properties and a deep understanding of your target market. Establish a strong working relationship to gain valuable insights and access to potential deals.

Example: When investing in a rapidly growing city like Austin, Texas, work with a local agent who understands which neighborhoods are experiencing the most growth and can guide you toward properties with high appreciation potential.

Chapter 5: Analyzing Investment Properties

Financial Analysis Tools

Conducting a thorough financial analysis is crucial for assessing the viability of an investment property. Here are some key considerations:

- **Cash Flow**: Calculate your monthly cash flow by subtracting all expenses (mortgage, taxes, insurance, maintenance, and property management fees) from your rental income. Ensure the cash flow is positive and aligns with your investment goals.

- **Profitability**: Consider the property's long-term profitability by evaluating potential rental income increases and property appreciation. Analyze your cash-on-cash return, which measures the return on your investment based on the cash you've invested.

Investment Metrics

- **Return on Investment (ROI)**: Calculate ROI by dividing the net profit from the investment by the initial investment cost. Compare this figure to benchmarks or other investment options to assess potential profitability.
- **Internal Rate of Return (IRR)**: Use IRR to evaluate the investment's profitability over

time. This metric considers the time value of money and provides a more comprehensive view of potential returns.

Case Studies and Examples

Let's look at a real-life example. Jane invested in a duplex in a suburban neighborhood. She purchased the property for $200,000, with a $40,000 down payment. After calculating expenses and rental income, her monthly cash flow was $400. Over five years, the property appreciated, and Jane's ROI was 15% annually.

Chapter 6: Managing Rental Properties

Property Management Options

Effective property management is crucial for maintaining your investment and ensuring positive cash flow. You can choose to self-manage your properties or hire a professional property manager.

- **Self-Management**: If you have the time and skills, self-management can save money and give you direct control over tenant interactions and maintenance decisions. However, it requires significant effort and a hands-on approach.
- **Hiring a Property Manager**: A property manager handles day-to-day operations, including tenant communication, rent collection, and maintenance. This option is ideal for investors who prefer a more passive approach. When selecting a manager, ensure they have a good reputation and experience with properties similar to yours.

Tenant Screening and Leasing

Successful rental investments depend on finding and retaining quality tenants. Develop a thorough tenant screening process, including credit checks, background checks, and interviews. Define your ideal tenant profile based on rental history, income, and references.

Drafting a comprehensive lease agreement is essential for protecting your investment. Include clauses covering rent payments, security deposits, maintenance responsibilities, and lease termination procedures.

Handling Maintenance and Repairs

Budgeting for maintenance costs is critical to maintaining the property's value and ensuring tenant satisfaction. Establish a reserve fund for unexpected repairs and routine maintenance. Build a network of reliable contractors and service providers for quick and efficient responses to maintenance issues.

Example: John owns a multi-family property with ten units. He budgets 10% of his rental income for maintenance and keeps a list of trusted plumbers, electricians, and handymen to address issues promptly. This proactive approach minimizes tenant complaints and enhances property value.

Chapter 7: Tax Strategies and Legal Considerations

Understanding Real Estate Tax Benefits

Real estate investments offer several tax advantages that can significantly enhance returns. These include:

- **Depreciation**: Deducting the cost of the property over its useful life reduces taxable income.

- **Interest Deductions**: Mortgage interest is tax-deductible, lowering your overall tax liability.
- **Expense Write-Offs**: Deductible expenses include property management fees, repairs, and travel costs related to property management.

1031 Exchanges

A 1031 exchange allows you to defer capital gains taxes by reinvesting proceeds from a property sale into a similar property. This strategy helps investors grow their portfolios without immediate tax liabilities. Work with a qualified intermediary to ensure compliance with IRS regulations.

Legal Aspects of Rental Properties

Understanding landlord-tenant laws is crucial for avoiding legal disputes and protecting your investment. Familiarize yourself with regulations regarding lease agreements, eviction procedures, and   tenant rights in your area.

Consider setting up a Limited Liability Company (LLC) to own your properties.   An LLC can offer liability protection,   separating personal and business assets   and reducing personal exposure to legal risks.

Insurance

Securing appropriate insurance coverage is essential to safeguard your   investment.
Consider the following types of insurance:

- **Property Insurance**: Protects against physical damage to the property.
- **Liability Insurance**: Covers legal costs if someone is injured on your property.

- **Loss of Income Insurance**: Compensates for lost rental income due to property damage.

Chapter 8: Scaling Your Real Estate Portfolio

Strategies for Growth

Once you've established a solid foundation, you can scale your real estate portfolio to achieve greater wealth and financial independence. Consider these strategies:

- **Leveraging Equity**: Use equity from existing properties to finance additional investments.

Refinancing or using a home equity line of credit can provide funds for new purchases.

- **Reinvesting Profits**: Channel rental income into acquiring more properties or improving existing ones, thereby increasing cash flow and property value.
- **Partnerships and Joint Ventures**: Pooling resources with other investors can expand your purchasing power and diversify your portfolio. Ensure clear agreements are in place to manage responsibilities and profit sharing.

Portfolio Management

Balancing different types of properties and geographic locations is crucial for managing risk and optimizing returns. Regularly monitor the performance of your portfolio and adjust strategies as needed. Consider factors like changing market conditions, tenant demographics, and economic forecasts.

Example: Sarah began with a single-family rental property and reinvested her profits to acquire additional properties over several years. By diversifying into multi-family units and commercial properties, she achieved financial independence and built a robust portfolio that weathered market fluctuations.

Conclusion

Building Long-Term Wealth with Real Estate

Real estate offers unparalleled opportunities for building long-term wealth and achieving financial goals. With the right strategies, investors can benefit from compounding growth, passive income, and property appreciation. Whether you're starting with one rental property or expanding a portfolio, real estate can be a powerful tool for creating lasting financial security.

Continuing Education and Resources

Investing in real estate is a journey of continuous learning. Stay informed about market trends, tax changes, and investment strategies to adapt to evolving conditions. Explore further reading, online courses, and real estate investment groups for ongoing education and support.

Final Thoughts and Encouragement

Embarking on a real estate investment journey can be both exciting and challenging. Remember, every successful investor started somewhere. With dedication, research, and strategic planning, you can achieve your investment goals and build a prosperous future. Take the first step today, and let real estate be your pathway to financial freedom.

Appendices

Glossary of Terms

- **Cap Rate**: A metric used to evaluate the return potential of a real estate investment, calculated by dividing the net operating income by the property's purchase price.
- **Cash Flow**: The net income from a property after all expenses have been paid.

Useful Resources and Tools

- **Websites**: Zillow, Redfin, and Realtor.com for property listings and market data.
- **Books**: "Rich Dad Poor Dad" by Robert Kiyosaki for foundational investment principles.

Sample Financial Analysis Worksheets

- **Cash Flow Worksheet**: Calculate monthly income and expenses to assess profitability.
- **ROI Calculator**: Determine the return on investment for potential properties.

Checklist for Property Evaluation

1. Analyze market trends and economic indicators.
2. Assess location and proximity to amenities.
3. Evaluate property condition and potential renovation costs.
4. Consider historical price trends and future development plans.